edition taberna kritika

Die edition taberna kritika wird vom Bundesamt für Kultur (CH) mit einem Förderbeitrag für die Jahre 2021–2024 unterstützt.

Hartmut Abendschein
Concrete Strategies

© edition taberna kritika, Bern (2023)
http://www.etkbooks.com/
Gestaltung: etkbooks, Bern
Coverillustration: Hartmut Abendschein

Bibliografische Information der Deutschen Nationalbibliothek: Die Deutsche Nationalbibliothek verzeichnet diese Publikation in der Deutschen Nationalbibliografie; detaillierte bibliografische Daten sind im Internet über http://www.dnb.de abrufbar.

ISBN: 978-3-905846-70-6

Hartmut Abendschein

Concrete Strategies

Übungen mit den "Oblique Strategies"
Exercises on "Oblique Strategies"

edition taberna kritika

Concrete Strategies
Übungen mit den "Oblique Strategies"

Eine Übung pro Tag in weniger als 5 Minuten – durchgeführt mit Google Docs (Ausnahmen mit * gekennzeichnet). Diese 114 Übungen folgen einer alphabetisierten Liste der Originaltexte von Brian Eno und Peter Schmidt (1975ff.). Die dort notierte Strategie wird dabei jeweils auf ihre eigene Textlichkeit angewendet und mutiert zum konkreten Gedicht.

Concrete Strategies
Exercises on "Oblique Strategies"

An exercise a day in less than 5 minutes – done with Google Docs (exceptions marked with *). These 114 exercises follow an alphabetised list of the original texts by Brian Eno and Peter Schmidt (1975ff.). The strategy noted there is applied in each case to its own textuality and mutates into a concrete poem.

09-12.2022

Aban on normal
inst ent

advice

Accretion

has

two

sites

easement

Are there sections ? Consider transitions

Please work
against your better
judgement!

body?

Assemble   the instruments
some of   in a

gro
up

and treat
the group

Balance
the
consistency
principle

inconsistency
principle
the
with

dirty

Brea

the

mo

re

deep

ly

- build -
B ridge s   b

urn

Cascades

i   u

n   s   m   e

    t   r   n   t

onthing
immaculate
consistency

ˈtʃɪldrənz ˈvɔɪsɪz

♪ ˈtʃɪldrənz ˈvɔɪsɪz

s
l u   ana
C te
r   s
ly si

Consider

different

fading

Consult[1] other[2] sources[3]

--

[1] promising
[2] unpromising
[3]

element

----

element

CouRAGE!

Cut a vital

con

nection

Dd

e e

c c

o r , r o

a a

t t

ee

De

fine an area as

S

A

F

and   E   use

it as an an

chor

-ionghnt

prtntog-omnthe
iihtm tsa

Axiom

desire

them

Discover

the recipes

you are using and abandon

time

n o t h i n g

things

/

easy

o

Don't   f

                              c

        tened   li

                              ch

be frigh   e

              s

Don't be

frightened

to display your

[si*l*ence]

Don't stress

<u>one thing</u>

more than

<u>another</u>

something boring something boring

D
h e
w a s
h i n
g u p
Ot

Do the changings need word?

Do we need holes?

*diff*erenceS

repetitions

the
flavs

CHOICE

45

e b k   t s u i

F d c e c   **O**rdings int **O** an acous c t t n

e a r   i i a o

everysomethingbeat

y

massaged

ou

r ne

c k

Ghost

Ghost

Ghost

Ghost

Ghost

Ghost

Ghost

Ghost

t h e
--- --- --- --- --- ---
game

worst

i

m

p

u

l

s

e

Go slowly

the outside all

the way round

Honor[3] as a hidden intention

How?

something

:-)

themusic:

th

e   mu

sic

Infinitesimal gradation

credib

nob

hum

ility

Into the
imp

ssible

?

finished

Is

it

Is there some missing?

tuning =/≠
appropriate

Just carry on

channel   channel
channel

Listen

Lis
ten quiet
to voice
the

a very s**m**all object

the othingsrder

the most
embarrassing details
them

beat   riff

single

note

an

exquisite

blank

frame

- e
- v
- e
- r
- y
- t
- h
- i
- n
- g
- the last thing

a
c
t
i n
corporate
n

s o   m e
            idiosyncratic
th i   n g

M   u   con

     t   ti

e   &   nue

kind kind kind kind kind kind kind
kind kind kind kind kind kind kind
kind kind kind kind kind kind kind
kind kind kind kind kind kind kind
kind kind kind kind kind kind kind
kind kind kind kind kind kind kind
kind kind kind kind kind kind kind
kind kind kind kind kind kind kind
kind kind kind kind kind kind kind
kind kind kind kind kind kind kind
kind kind kind kind kind kind kind
kind kind kind kind kind kind kind
kind kind

Org   nic

(a   )

mac   ery

hin

resist change

tly

earPutplugs

those

quiet

evenings

specifics

specifics

change change change change change
change change change change change
change change change change change
change change change change change
change change change change change
change change change change change
change change change change change
change change change change change
change change change change change
change change change change change
change change change change change
change change change change change
change change change change change
change change change change change

esreveR

*

a man eating peas with the idea that they will improve his virility shovels them straight into his lap

listen

Shut

t h e

door

-Simple

S   e   t   u
  p   c   r   m

T   b
a   r
k   e
e   a
a   k

in

of

apparent

non-

order

importance

your
mouth

The principle
inconsistency

Tibetan tape

the music

Think of the radi

u

p

n
the Trust O you
W

*

97

97

*

the spine

ἰδέα

fe e

filt
ers

'eelopp'

just now
y
u

istuation

mystakes

what

closest

friend

~~W~~hat

Work

Work

Work

<u>Work</u>

~~Work~~

Work

Work

tIme

r own
ideas

card

1. Abandon normal instruments
2. Accept advice
3. Accretion
4. A line has two sides
5. Allow an easement (an easement is the abandonment of a stricture)
6. Are there sections? Consider transitions
7. Ask people to work against their better judgement
8. Ask your body
9. Assemble some of the instruments in a group and treat the group
10. Balance the consistency principle with the inconsistency principle
11. Be dirty
12. Breathe more deeply
13. Bridges -build - burn
14. Cascades
15. Change instrument roles
16. Change nothing and continue with immaculate consistency
17. Children's voices - speaking -singing
18. Cluster analysis
19. Consider different fading systems
20. Consult other sources -promising -unpromising
21. Convert a melodic element into a rhythmic element
22. Courage!
23. Cut a vital connection
24. Decorate, decorate
25. Define an area as `safe' and use it as an anchor
26. Destroy -nothing - the most important thing
27. Discard an axiom
28. Disconnect from desire
29. Discover the recipes you are using and abandon them
30. Distorting time
31. Do nothing for as long as possible
32. Don't be afraid of things because they're easy to do
33. Don't be frightened of cliches
34. Don't be frightened to display your talents
35. Don't break the silence
36. Don't stress one thing more than another
37. Do something boring
38. Do the washing up
39. Do the words need changing?
40. Do we need holes?
41. Emphasize differences
42. Emphasize repetitions
43. Emphasize the flaws
44. Faced with a choice, do both (given by Dieter Rot)
45. Feedback recordings into an acoustic situation
46. Fill every beat with something
47. Get your neck massaged
48. Ghost echoes
49. Give the game away
50. Give way to your worst impulse
51. Go slowly all the way round the outside
52. Honor thy error as a hidden intention
53. How would you have done it?
54. Humanize something free of error
55. Imagine the music as a moving chain or caterpillar
56. Imagine the music as a set of disconnected events
57. Infinitesimal gradations
58. Intentions - credibility of - nobility of - humility of
59. Into the impossible
60. Is it finished?
61. Is there something missing?

62. Is Ihe tuning appropriate?
63. Just carry on
64. Left channel, right channel, centre channel
65. Listen in total darkness, or in a very !arge room, very quietly
66. Listen to lhe quiet voice
67. Look al a very small object, look at its centre
68. Look at the order in which you do things
69. Look closely at the most emba.rrassing details and amplify them
70. Lowest common denominator check -single beat - single note -single riff
71. Make a blank valuable by putting it in an exquisite frame
72. Makean exhauslive list of everything you might do and do the last thing on the list
73. Make a sudden, destructive llllpredictable action; incorporate
74. Mechanicalize something idiosyncratic
75. Mute and conlinue
76. Only one element of each kind
77. (Organic) machinery
78. Overtly resist cha.nge
79. Put in earplugs
80. Remember those quiel evenings
81. Remove ambiguilies and convert to specifks
82. Remove specitics and convert to ambiguities
83. Repetition is a form of change
84. Reverse
85. Shorl circuit (example: a man eating peas wilh tlle idea tllat they will improve his virility shovels tllem straight into his lap)
86. Shut the door and listen from outside
87. Simple subtraclion
88. Spectrum analysis
89. Take a break
90. Take away the elements in order of apparent non-importance
91. Tape your mouth (given by Rilva Saarikko)
92. The inconsistency principle
93. The tape is now themusic
94. Thi.nk of the radio
95. Tidyup
96. Trust in the you of now
97. Turn it upside down
98. Twist the spine
99. Use an old idea
100. Use an unacceplable color
101. Use fewer notes
102. Use filters
103. Use 'unqualified' people
104. Water
105. What are you really thinking about just now? Incorporate
106. What is the reality of the situation?
107. Vvhat mistakes did you make last time?
108. \'vhat would your closest friend do?
109. What wouldn't you do?
110. Work at a different spccd
111. Youarean engineer
112. You can only make one dot at a time
113. You don't have to be ashamed of using your own ideas
114. [blank white card]

Oblique Strategies - Over One Hundred Wortl1while Dilemmas
Brian Eno und Peter Schmidt (1975ff.)
More: https://en.wikipedia.org/wiki/Obliq ue_Strategies

Biographisches

Hartmut Abendschein (*1969): Aufgewachsen in Schwäbisch Hall, Buchhändler in Stuttgart, Studium der Germanistik und Anglistik in Konstanz und Glasgow, wiss. Dokumentar in Köln, lebt und arbeitet in Bern. Publikationen (Auswahl): Die Träume meiner Frau (2007). Bibliotheca Caelestis (2008). The Chomskytree-Haiku (Rhizome(Rhizome)) (2011). Dranmor. Roman (2012). Schellendiskursli / Schellenexkursli (2013). Recycling Le Tour de France (2014). Flarf Disco. Popgedichte (2015). nicht begonnenes fortsetzen. Text, Kontur, Schatten (2017). mn ltztr krnz ei ee a (2019). Author DNA (2019). asemic walks (2020). Hartmann. Stempelroman (2021). bricolages. Konzeptuelle und visuelle Dichtungen, Objekte (2022). Mehr: www.abendschein.ch

edition taberna kritika
Neuerscheinungen 2022/23

Christian de Simoni
wandern / schreiben
ISBN 978-3-905846-69-0

Bojan Savić Ostojić
Punkt
ISBN 978-3-905846-68-3

Hannes Bajohr
Renga Anger
ISBN 978-3-905846-67-6

Daniele Pantano
HIMMEL-BIMMEL-BAM-BAM
ISBN 978-3-905846-66-9

Jasmin Meerhoff
Knoten und Bäuche
ISBN 978-3-905846-65-2

Sebastian Winkler
texere [weben]
ISBN 978-3-905846-64-5

Ausführliche Informationen über unsere
Neuerscheinungen und das Gesamtprogramm finden Sie im
Internet unter www.etkbooks.com

edition taberna kritika
Gutenbergstrasse 47
CH - 3011 Bern
Tel.: +41 (0) 77 425 2 180
info@etkbooks.com | http://www.etkbooks.com